·········· 🏠 ··········

Homeless or Hopeless?

MARGERY G. NICHELASON

LERNER PUBLICATIONS COMPANY

MINNEAPOLIS

For Jan and Amy

Copyright © 1994 Lerner Publications Company

All rights reserved. International copyright secured. No part of this book may be reproduced, stored in a retrieval system, or transmitted in any form or by any means, electronic, mechanical, photocopying, recording, or otherwise, without the prior written permission of Lerner Publications Company, except for the inclusion of brief quotations in an acknowledged review.

Library of Congress Cataloging-in-Publication Data

Nichelason, Margery G.
    Homeless or Hopeless/Margery G. Nichelason.
        p. cm. — (Pro/Con)
    Includes bibliographical references and index.
    Summary: Examines the problem of homelessness in the United States, including its causes and effects, society's responsibilities, and government and private assistance programs.
    ISBN 0-8225-2606-9
    1. Homelessness—United States—Juvenile literature. [1. Homelessness. 2. Homeless persons.] I. Title   II. Series.
HV4505.N53 1993
362.5—dc20   92-19675
                                                             CIP
                                                              AC

Manufactured in the United States of America

1 2 3 4 5 6 – I/JR – 99 98 97 96 95 94

CONTENTS

FOREWORD

If a nation expects to be ignorant and free, ... it expects what never was and never will be.

Thomas Jefferson

Are you ready to participate in forming the policies of our government? Many issues are very confusing, and it can be difficult to know what to think about them or how to make a decision about them. Sometimes you must gather information about a subject before you can be informed enough to make a decision. Bernard Baruch, a prosperous American financier and an advisor to every president from Woodrow Wilson to Dwight D. Eisenhower, said, "If you can get all the facts, your judgment can be right; if you don't get all the facts, it can't be right."

But gathering information is only one part of the decision-making process. The way you interpret information is influenced by the values you have been taught since infancy–ideas about right and wrong, good and bad. Many of your values are shaped, or at least influenced, by how and where you grow up, by your race, sex, and religion, by how much money your family has. What your parents believe, what they read, and what you read and believe influence your decisions. The values of friends and teachers also affect what you think.

It's always good to listen to the opinions of people around you, but you will often confront contradictory points of view and points of view that are based not on fact, but on myth. John F. Kennedy, the 35th president of the United States, said, "The great enemy of the truth is very often not the lie–deliberate, contrived, and dishonest–

4

but the myth–persistent, persuasive, and unrealistic." Eventually you will have to separate fact from myth and make up your own mind, make your own decisions. Because you are responsible for your decisions, it's important to get as much information as you can. Then your decisions will be the right ones for you.

Making a fair and informed decision can be an exciting process, a chance to examine new ideas and different points of view. You live in a world that changes quickly and sometimes dramatically– a world that offers the opportunity to explore the ever-changing ground between yourself and others. Instead of forming a single, easy, or popular point of view, you might develop a rich and complex vision that offers new alternatives. Explore the many dimensions of an idea. Find kinship among an extensive range of opinions. Only after you've done this should you try to form your own opinions.

After you have formed an opinion about a particular subject, you may believe it is the only right decision. But some people will disagree with you and challenge your beliefs. They are not trying to antagonize you or put you down. They probably believe that they're right as sincerely as you believe you are. Thomas Macaulay, an English historian and author, wrote, "Men are never so likely to settle a question rightly as when they discuss it freely." In a democracy, the free exchange of ideas is not only encouraged, it's vital. Examining and discussing public issues and understanding opposing ideas are desirable and necessary elements of a free nation's ability to govern itself.

This Pro/Con series is designed to explore and examine different points of view on contemporary issues and to help you develop an understanding and appreciation of them. Most importantly, it will help you form your own opinions and make your own honest, informed decisions.

Mary Winget
Series Editor

5

This child and his family live in a camping trailer.

AN OVERVIEW

Richard has attended three different schools this year, and it's only January. He does his homework in the bathroom—the only quiet place in the church basement that serves as a shelter for homeless families like his.

Five-year-old Sarah sleeps on the back floor of a beat-up 1978 Buick Le Sabre—home for four people. All night long, the bump in the middle of the floor pushes into her back. All of her family's possessions are in the trunk of the car.

Eleven-year-old Sam lived with his father in an abandoned school bus for a month. After they used up their food stamps, their meals consisted of ketchup and mustard. At night, when temperatures fell below freezing, they slept on a foam mattress. By the time the state police were alerted, Sam was suffering from malnutrition and a severe case of frostbite, and both his feet had to be amputated. Sam's father told authorities that the state agency he had approached for assistance refused to help him, except for providing $60 in food stamps—and that had been two months ago.

These children are just a few of the many homeless people in the United States. Estimates of the number of homeless people vary enormously and depend on how homelessness is defined, who is doing the counting, and the method used in the count.

In 1983 the Department of Health and Human Services (HHS)—a part of the executive branch of the federal government that deals with public health, social welfare, and income security—estimated that there might be as many as 2 million homeless people in the United States.[1] The following year, the Department of Housing and Urban Development (HUD) proposed a much lower estimate of 250,000 to 350,000.[2] In yet another report, the National Coalition for the Homeless (NCH), an advocacy group, estimated the number of homeless people to be between 1.5 and 3 million.[3]

All existing estimates are open to criticism, however, because most of the homeless are not counted in the Census of Population or in the Current Population Survey. Counting them is extremely difficult. Again, the way in which a study is conducted and who is conducting it seem to affect its outcome.

The way homelessness is defined affects the count as well. If the definition of homelessness is limited to those living in shelters and on the street, the count will be lower. If it includes those who are inadequately housed—those living in vacant buildings, for example—and those who are living with friends or family members, the number will be greater.

Advocacy groups, such as the NCH, who plead the cause of the homeless, are often accused of inflating their numbers, thus making the problem seem worse than it really is. On the other hand, many advocacy groups believe the HUD criteria are too narrow and fail to count many homeless people. Whether the numbers fall at the high end or the low end of the spectrum, however, they point to a serious national problem.

Homelessness is not a new problem, but it has become more severe in recent years, and certain aspects of it have changed dramatically. During the Great Depression of the 1930s, for example, the Federal Emergency Relief Administration set up camps for homeless transients—people who move frequently from one place to another and seldom remain in one location long enough to become known. Other people who were homeless during the depression lived in shantytowns—areas of crude housing made from scraps of wood, metal, cardboard, or whatever could be found. In general, people had little sympathy for the homeless, most of whom were young men moving from place to place in search of a job. When the United States entered World War II in 1941, the number of homeless dropped significantly. Many young men joined the armed forces or worked in defense industries—companies that make arms and other supplies for the military.

When the war ended in 1945, employment remained high and the rate of homelessness remained low, but the makeup of the homeless population changed. In contrast to prewar years, most of the homeless during the 1950s and 1960s were middle-aged to older men. In urban areas, they generally congregated on the Skid Rows of the nation—neighborhoods with cheap hotels, bars, restaurants, and religious missions. In fact, only a small number actually slept on the streets. Most of these homeless men lived in cheap SRO (single-room occupancy) hotels, where they could rent small rooms for 50 to 90 cents a night. Although such places could hardly be called homes, they did provide shelter and some privacy.

Almost all of the men who lived on Skid Row worked in menial, low-paying jobs at least occasionally. About 25 percent of them lived on Social Security pensions, monthly checks sent to them by the federal government. Almost all the men (90 percent) were white, 25 percent were alcoholic, 20 percent were mentally ill, 20 percent

Because there is no more room in the SRO (single-room occupancy) hotel, this man will spend the night on the street.

*Shantytowns, such as the one in New York City's Central Park
(top), were a common sight during the Great Depression of the
1930s, and they have recently reappeared in many large cities.
On-the-street homelessness has increased since the 1970s
(bottom).*

suffered from a physical disability, and 10 percent were "socially maladjusted."[4] Of course, the categories overlapped in many cases, so one individual could be a white alcoholic who was socially maladjusted. For the most part, the public paid little attention to these homeless men. Skid Rows were concentrated in urban areas that most people intentionally avoided—and also ignored.

In the mid-1970s, the composition of the homeless population shifted again. Congress approved more generous benefits for the elderly, as well as more money for programs that aided the physically disabled and the mentally ill. Those payments greatly reduced the number of Skid Row residents. Also, as metropolitan areas expanded, parking lots, office buildings, and apartments replaced SRO hotels. Nearly half the SRO units in this country were lost, about one million in all.[5] At the same time, crimes such as public drunkenness, loitering, and vagrancy were decriminalized, which meant that police patrols were no longer arresting homeless alcoholics and taking them to jail. By the late 1970s, the "old" homeless were being replaced by the "new" homeless—a younger group that also began to include more women and children. On-the-street homelessness increased, and the face of homelessness began to change yet again and to become more visible to the public.

A recession in the early 1980s caused unemployment to rise as high as 9.7 percent, and almost 11 million workers lost their jobs, including many in highly skilled professions.[6] Many people who were already poverty-stricken slipped into homelessness or moved in with members of their families, a practice known as "doubling up." In 1983, 17,000 families were illegally dou-

The "new" homeless have become more visible than their predecessors.

bled up in New York City's public housing. By 1986 the number had climbed to 35,000. If private as well as public housing is counted, the number of families that were doubled up jumps to 100,000 by November 1986.[7]

During this same decade, the federal government—under the leadership of presidents Ronald Reagan and George Bush—dramatically decreased the budget for low-income housing. The budget fell from more than $30 billion in 1981 to $6.7 billion in 1990. Public housing construction dropped from 30,000 units in 1982 to about 2,200 in 1987. In the early 1990s, almost one million people were on waiting lists for public housing.[8] In the meantime, many of them were homeless.

The new homeless, those who have become homeless since the late 1970s, are no longer concentrated on Skid Row, and almost half of them are literally on the streets

Many homeless people temporarily double up with family or friends.

and without shelter. They are visible throughout the downtown areas of all major cities. Only about one-fifth of America's homeless are found in rural areas.[9] Significant numbers of women and children are counted among the new homeless, and the homeless population is younger—primarily in their 20s and 30s—than their Skid Row counterparts. Also, fewer of the new homeless are employed. Their incomes are generally about $100.00 per month or $3.25 per day. (The cheapest hotels cost at least $5.00 per day, and a round-trip bus fare in major cities costs $2.00 to $3.00.) The ethnic composition of the homeless population has also changed. Minority groups among the homeless reflect the ethnic mix of the general population of an area, but blacks account for more than 50 percent of the homeless in many large cities.[10]

Although the homeless have become quite visible on city streets, many others remain invisible—some because they choose to be. They feel embarrassed or ashamed of their homelessness and try to hide or disguise their situation. Other homeless people suffer from mental disorders that make them suspicious of strangers. Such people may prefer to live secluded lives under bridges or in abandoned buildings rather than interact with other people. Shelters and programs are of little use to them.

Lifestyle can also affect visibility. For example, many homeless people stay in one city for years, while others are transients who never stay in one spot for very long. Those who live doubled up with family or friends often

Some homeless people prefer solitude to shelter.

do not appear to be homeless—and often are not counted as homeless—because they have an address and a place to stay temporarily. They are, however, considered by others to be homeless, because they have no permanent residence, and they can be told to leave their temporary residence at any time.

Many people, when thinking of the homeless, have a stereotypical image—that is, they expect the homeless to look and behave a certain way. For example, a reporter in Washington, D.C., wanted to interview some homeless people who, he had been told, lived in Lafayette Square, a park across the street from the White House. When he walked through the park, however, he could not find any homeless individuals. Although more than 20 were present, he didn't recognize them as being homeless because they didn't fit the stereotypical image.[11]

When you think of a homeless person, what image comes to mind? Do you picture a toothless old woman, a "bag lady," pushing her possessions around in a shopping cart or carrying them in shopping bags? Or perhaps an unkempt man, a "wino," drinking cheap liquor from a bottle stuck inside a brown paper bag? Or a filthy person sleeping on a sidewalk or in a doorway? Such images do describe many of the homeless, but definitely not all of them. Many of the homeless are young women with children; people who have been laid off work and can't find another job; victims of natural disasters such as floods and fires; or runaways and "throwaways"—teenagers who have run away from or been thrown out of their homes. The HUD "1988 National Survey of Shelters for the Homeless" breaks down the homeless population as follows:

Are these men homeless or just relaxing in a park?

Unaccompanied men	45%
Unaccompanied women	14%
Families	40%
People under age 18	26%
Mentally ill	34%
Physically disabled	11%
Domestic violence victims	21%[12]

These statistics reveal that homeless people often fit into more than one category. For example, Rosita is homeless. She is alone, fleeing home because her husband was abusive. In the HUD study, Rosita would be counted as both an unaccompanied woman and a domestic violence victim. Other statistics show that approximately 33 percent of the homeless have mental disorders, about 33 percent are chronic alcoholics, and about 20 percent use hard drugs.[13] Approximately 33 percent are veterans, mainly from the Vietnam War.[14]

Although in many other countries homelessness is far more widespread than in the United States, many Americans consider it a national disgrace in a country as rich and dedicated to human rights as ours. Others who look at homelessness in foreign countries—especially in developing countries—and compare it to homelessness in the United States do not see a crisis situation here. In fact, they point out that the United States has one of the lowest rates of homelessness in the world, so it should not be a high priority on our national agenda. They believe the problem has been blown out of proportion.

The problem of homelessness increasingly arouses both sympathy *and* anger among the general public. Many people are frustrated with the problem and are tired of being stopped on the street and asked to give money, or being forced to step over sleeping bodies lying in streets and storefronts. Some panhandlers have become quite bold and sometimes even threatening. Sarah Ferguson, a writer for Pacific News Service, reports of panhandlers in New York City's Greenwich Village who confront passersby with signs that read "Homeless Donations: $1 or token." She describes an increasingly familiar scene:

> "Cheap bastards," mutters one of the beggars, an African-American man named Flower, as he dumps on the sidewalk a handful of pennies that a passerby just gave him. "What am I supposed to do with that?"
>
> "Look, corporate criminals!" shouts his companion, Paradise, who sports preppy clothes and seashells woven in his short dreadlocks, pointing to a

A panhandler sits outside an opulent shop, as passersby window-shop.

group of businessmen picking up their Lincoln Continental in the parking lot next door. "Hello Mr. Executive, how you doing? You remember how to be human, don't you?" Paradise asks him mockingly, shoving a cardboard box in his face. "Come on, give me a dollar man, I bet you make $50,000 in 10 minutes," he shouts. In response, the driver edges his window down a crack and mutters, "Get a job, will you?"

Meanwhile, Flower is chasing a frightened-looking man on the street. "Help me out. I know you're afraid of black people, but I won't bite."

"Just because I have a suit on doesn't mean I'm a yuppie. I just lost my job."[15]

In many areas, an attitude of "Us vs. Them" has encouraged government efforts to get the homeless out of public view. Even in Berkeley, a California city known for its liberal politics, police have driven the vagrants and the dispossessed out of People's Park, which they

Some people want an alternate lifestyle and live on the streets by choice.

had come to think of as home. According to Ferguson, part of the reason for the growing backlash is sheer numbers. The number of substance abusers and able-bodied but unemployed men among the homeless population also contributes to the growing friction. Many people distinguish between what they consider the ''worthy'' and the ''unworthy'' poor. They feel little or no responsibility for homeless people who are on the streets by choice or because of problems they have probably brought on themselves, such as drug or alcohol abuse. They believe that it's time for such people to take responsibility for themselves.

In response, some homeless people are banding together in support networks such as the National Union

of the Homeless. This group is trying to organize homeless people across the country. They have also taken over
some abandoned government buildings in an effort to
force the government to turn them over to homeless
families. They insist that homeless people don't want
more shelters and welfare, they want homes and jobs.

As you can see, the issue of homelessness is more complex than it appears at first. The many factors and
sources that may contribute to an individual's mental
illness, alcoholism, or drug abuse, for example, may be
complicated and difficult to trace. Emphasizing different
aspects of the problem can influence how we view the
homeless, our sense of responsibility toward them, and
our feelings of compassion or antagonism. Our views,
in turn, influence our sense of responsibility toward the
homeless or lack thereof, and our willingness to help
them or to ignore them. Some people see only substance
abusers, unemployed men and women, and panhandlers.
Others point out the large number of intact families and
children on the streets, employable people who cannot
find jobs, and homeless people who are fully employed.

Who *are* the homeless, and what caused them to
become that way?

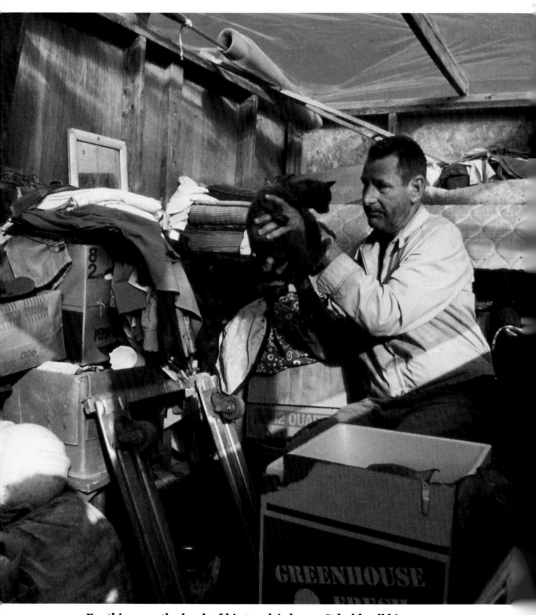

For this man, the back of his truck is home. It holds all his worldly possessions.

THE CAUSES OF HOMELESSNESS

Pam never thought she would be homeless. Her husband had worked as a window washer, but as his services became less and less in demand, he stayed home to care for their three children. Pam had a part-time job as a respiratory therapist in a hospital. Her job was supposed to turn into a full-time job, but instead the hospital laid off some employees, and Pam was among them. Two other hospitals in the city had recently closed, so Pam's job opportunities were limited. Suddenly the family had no income and could not pay its rent. In a hasty effort to find work, Pam's family put most of their belongings into storage and traveled to other cities in search of job opportunities. They lived in their van while they were traveling, but when it broke down in Cheyenne, Wyoming, Pam and her family were stranded. They had no money to fix the van, no money for a hotel or for bus tickets, and no credit cards. They had no friends or family members they could call for help. When Pam lost her job, she and her family quickly slipped from living comfortably in their own apartment to becoming homeless in a strange city.[1]

Loss of income is a frequent cause of homelessness, and Pam's story is not unusual. Income is an important factor in determining people's lifestyles—the kind of home they live in, the food they eat, the clothes they buy, the medical and dental care they get, and the types of entertainment they can enjoy. Since 1991 an income of $13,359 has been considered the poverty line for a family of four in the United States. The federal government considers families that earn less than that amount to be officially poor. In 1990 an estimated 33.6 million people lived in poverty in the United States.[2] Almost half the poor are children.[3]

Like Pam, many people fall into poverty and eventually risk homelessness because of job loss. Jeb, for example, was an assembly-line worker for an automobile manufacturer. When the economy slowed down, fewer people could afford to buy new cars, so Jeb and many other workers were laid off. Because he was supporting a wife and three children, Jeb anxiously applied for work at other companies, but few jobs were available, and many people wanted them. He used his savings for day-to-day living expenses, but eventually that money ran out. Without an income, Jeb and his family became destitute and faced homelessness.

An increasing number of people are finding themselves in situations like Pam's and Jeb's. According to the American Federation of Labor and Congress of Industrial Organizations (AFL–CIO), since 1979 there has been a yearly loss of two million jobs in manufacturing industries (such as textiles and steel)—jobs that paid good wages.[4] Furthermore, the General Accounting Office found that between 1979 and 1984 only half the laid-off

Having a job is an important difference between the man on the right and the other men in the picture.

workers had found other employment two years after losing their jobs. Those that did find new jobs earned only 70 percent of their previous wages.[5] According to author Peter Marin, in any homeless shelter, you can find women and men who have worked for 10, 20, or 40 years but still end up homeless.[6]

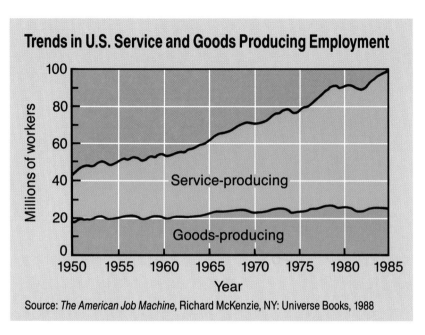

Trends in U.S. Service and Goods Producing Employment

Service-producing

Goods-producing

Source: *The American Job Machine*, Richard McKenzie, NY: Universe Books, 1988

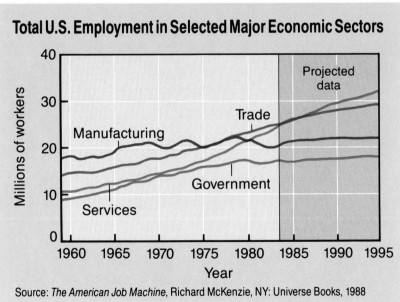

Total U.S. Employment in Selected Major Economic Sectors

Projected data

Trade

Manufacturing

Government

Services

Source: *The American Job Machine*, Richard McKenzie, NY: Universe Books, 1988

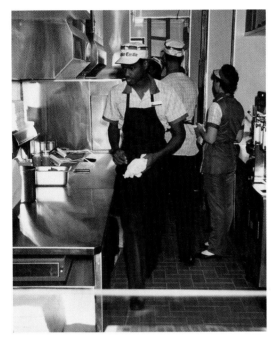

Minimum-wage service jobs, top left, are replacing well-paying manufacturing jobs, bottom, at an alarming rate.

Many poor and homeless people work full-time (40 hours a week) but are underemployed. In other words, they are working, but they don't make enough money to get above the poverty line. In 1986, two million adults were poor even though they worked full-time.[7] In 1987 the United States Conference of Mayors estimated that 22 percent of the homeless were employed on a full- or part-time basis but still didn't earn enough to pay their bills.[8] This situation arises, in part, because as manufacturing jobs disappear, they are being replaced mostly by low-paying service jobs. Many working Americans are earning the minimum wage—the lowest hourly rate that employers can pay their workers. Since April 1, 1991, people working at minimum-wage jobs have been paid $4.25 an hour.[9]

Tim, for example, flips hamburgers at a fast-food restaurant. Working full-time for a year at minimum wage, he will earn less than $9,000—from which taxes are deducted. If Tim lives at home with his parents, his earnings might easily provide for his needs. But if Tim is supporting a wife and two children, his family is in trouble because Tim's salary is well below the poverty level. It will be difficult—if not impossible—for Tim to meet his family's basic needs of food, clothing, and shelter. When people are in poverty, making housing payments often becomes their first big difficulty. They may move to cheaper and cheaper housing, but eventually they cannot even manage the cheapest housing— and they become homeless.

In 1989 the Low-Income Housing Information Service, a group committed to educating the public about housing for the poor, studied the availability of low-income housing. The study revealed that in 44 states, two wage earners could work full-time at minimum-wage jobs and still not be able to afford a moderately priced, one-bedroom apartment. A two-bedroom apartment was beyond the reach of such wage earners in all 50 states.[10] Opportunities for jobs that pay more than minimum wage are decreasing. Between 1979 and 1988, almost three-fourths of the new jobs created were service and sales jobs, which usually offer workers low wages and few benefits. Higher-paying manufacturing jobs, even for skilled workers, are dwindling. If this trend continues, by the year 2000 almost half the jobs in the United States could pay employees less money than is needed to cover the cost of their housing.[11]

At the same time that many people are earning less, inflation is decreasing the purchasing value of the dollars they have. If prices rise, the money a person earns will buy fewer and fewer goods and services. If the cost of housing, heating, clothing, food, medical care, day care, and other necessities continues to rise, more families may be forced to choose among basic needs. Some people must choose whether to feed and house their family or to pay the heating bill.

Inflation also affects elderly people because they live on fixed incomes—incomes that remain at the same level regardless of inflation. Each month many senior citizens receive money from sources such as Social Security, other government programs, and private retirement pensions. When the cost of goods and services rises, however, many elderly Americans must use their limited funds for food and medicine instead of for rent or house payments.

The majority of people who live in extreme poverty do not end up on the street.[12] Most people, even the very poor, have someone or someplace to turn to in times of hardship—friends, family members, private charities, a church, or a synagogue. People who end up on the street are often isolated from friends and family, and friction often exists between the homeless and their relatives. In fact, some experts define homelessness in part as a state of "disaffiliation"—a state of life without enduring and supporting ties to family or friends.[13] Disaffiliation distinguishes the homeless on the street from those who are living in extreme poverty but under the roof of a friend or family member.

Some people could avoid homelessness by making use of benefits that already exist under various government

This woman has no one to turn to for help.

Suffering from mental illness, this man is incapable of caring for himself.

programs, but they are not capable of applying for benefits. For example, approximately a third of the homeless are mentally ill and cannot adequately care for themselves.[14] Until the mid-1960s, most of the mentally ill were cared for in state mental institutions, where they had around-the-clock care and supervision. During the 1960s, caregivers searched for more humane and effective ways of treating the mentally ill, partially out of concern for their patients' civil rights. Their efforts resulted in a plan to transfer the care of mental patients from state institutions to community-based mental health centers. Instead of being institutionalized, mentally ill people who were not considered a threat to themselves or others could live in their homes and receive outpatient care (care given through regular visits rather than admission) at mental health centers in their own communities—a system that would also save taxpayers' money. As a result, thousands of mentally ill people were released from mental institutions with the promise of support from community mental health centers.[15]

Unfortunately, this "deinstitutionalization" process didn't work because only 800 of the 2,500 planned community mental health centers were built.[16] Patients were released from state mental institutions with their small bundles of belongings, a week's worth of medicine, and bus fare. Many who had no place to go and no one to go to ended up on the streets.

Between 1980 and 1988, the federal government reduced the amount of money spent to support community mental health programs by almost a third,[17] making even less help available to homeless people like Jim. Before he became mentally ill, Jim was a government employee. Now he spends his nights on a cot at the Salvation Army and his days on his hands and knees digging in the dirt for imaginary gold. Jim cannot be committed to a mental institution because he is not considered dangerous to himself or others. Without help he is unable to care for himself, remaining harmless but homeless.

Some experts believe that because so many homeless people have long-term mental health problems, homelessness must be a problem of the mentally ill. C. Brandon Crocker, a financial planner in San Diego, California, quite logically argues that "addressing the problems of the mentally ill would go a long way in shrinking the homeless problem. Certainly, many people with mental disabilities are able to care for themselves outside of institutions. But it is also obvious...that those mentally ill people who are unable to hold down a job, make use of government services, and are otherwise unable to look after normal day-to-day functions which would keep them off the street do need to be institutionalized..."[18]

Others disagree, pointing out that the major wave of people leaving institutions occurred decades ago, well before homelessness soared to its current level. Furthermore, they reason, if homelessness is a mental health problem, what accounts for the two-thirds who are not mentally ill?

Although many have had homelessness forced on them because of the circumstances of their lives, others have chosen, at least in part, to live in the "marginal" world of the homeless, on the fringe of mainstream society. In some cases, they have even embraced a life of homelessness because they either reject the values of the conventional world, or they can't find a place in it. In an article for *Harper's*, Peter Marin points out that "there may indeed be people...who have seen so much of our world, or seen it so clearly, that to live in it becomes impossible." For those people, homelessness can be seen as a "mute, furious refusal, a self-imposed exile far less appealing to the rest of us than ordinary life, but better in...[their] terms." Marin writes, "Yes, many of those on the streets could be transformed, rehabilitated. But there are others whose lives have been irrevocably changed, damaged beyond repair, and who no longer want help, who no longer recognize the *need* for help, and whose experience in our world has made them want only to be left alone."[19]

There is no single reason that people become homeless. Some are alcoholics or drug addicts. Some have just been released from jail and have no job and nowhere to go. One family lost their home and all their possessions in a fire. Another person has AIDS, is unemployed, and cannot pay his medical bills. These are just a few of the many circumstances that can cause people to become homeless.

For some people, however, poverty is a way of life, and they make little or no effort to change their situation. Their grandparents were poor, their parents were poor, and now they are poor. They have come to look at their monthly welfare check and food stamps as a permanent income rather than as short-term assistance. Chances are that their children will also be poor unless the cycle of poverty can be broken.[20] Only a small fraction of poor people—the poorest of the poor—become homeless, however.

The one trait all homeless people have in common is that they lack a permanent place to live. Therefore, many experts point to the shortage of affordable housing as the root cause of homelessness. While people with money can usually choose the type of housing and neighborhood they want to live in, poor people have few choices. They must find places where the rent is cheap. Dwellings with low rent payments, known as low-income housing units, are usually found in old, run-down neighborhoods. These units are often classified as substandard, which means they may lack such basic conveniences as heat, electricity, hot and cold running water, and workable plumbing.

Currently there is only one low-income housing unit available for every two families that need one.[21] Part of this shortage is due to the fact that approximately half a million low-rent units are lost each year.[22] Some are torched by arsonists; others are abandoned. Land developers often purchase such dilapidated structures for renovation or to make way for newer, more modern buildings. In a process called gentrification, developers turn the run-down buildings into stylish living, shopping, and business areas.

At the same time that the supply of existing low-income housing units is diminishing, fewer new low-income housing units are being constructed. Between 1976 and 1982, approximately 166,000 federally subsidized low-income housing units were produced annually. Now fewer than 25,000 units are built each year because of cutbacks in federal housing subsidies (money given to the poor to assist with rental payments).[23] Changes in the tax laws also make it less profitable for builders to construct low-income housing.

As the low-income housing market shrinks and the rate of poverty grows, what will happen to Pam and other homeless people who cannot even afford monthly rent payments? They may get on a waiting list for a public housing unit, but there is often a waiting period of up to 12 years. What will her family do in the meantime?

*Finding a free meal can be a problem for the homeless, since
food is served on a "first come, first served" basis.*

"THREE HOTS
AND A COT"

Arnie was a hero in Vietnam, where he proudly served his country as a marine. By the time he returned home, however, Arnie's life had changed, and he no longer fit in with his family and former friends. The sounds of gunfire and people's screams filled his nightmares. Instead of getting psychiatric help, Arnie turned to alcohol to obliterate his memories. After a while, Arnie's bottle of liquor became the only thing that mattered in his life. He couldn't keep a job, his drinking problem drove his family and friends away, and he eventually ended up living on the street. Arnie and other veterans make up one-third to one-half of the homeless population in the United States.[1]

For many homeless people like Arnie, life is lived a day at a time, and the future consists of each day's search for "three hots and a cot," three meals and a place to sleep. Although many churches and private agencies offer meals for the poor on a regular basis, Arnie is sometimes lucky to get even one meal a day. Arnie is a panhandler who spends his money on liquor.

To take advantage of free meals, Arnie must know where they are served, get directions to those locations, and find some means of transportation or walk long distances. It is "first come, first served," and arriving late means an empty plate. Also, many centers will not serve intoxicated persons.

Breakfast may be offered at a homeless center, lunch at a church, and dinner at a mission for the homeless. Dinner Monday and Thursday may be served at one location, Tuesday and Wednesday at another. Keeping all this meal information straight is often more than Arnie can handle, especially when he's drunk. In many cities, there are no free meals served on the weekends, and homeless people have to make do. If liquor alone won't deaden Arnie's craving for food, he can forage in trash dumpsters behind restaurants and perhaps find a discarded hamburger patty or part of a sandwich.

For the homeless, finding "a cot"—a safe place to sleep—isn't easy either. Although some people double up with friends or relatives, such arrangements become stressful. After a few weeks or months, the homeless individual or family is often asked to leave. Many people have no one with whom they can double up in the first place.

Once they're on the street, many homeless people turn to shelters for help. Most large cities have both public and privately owned shelters that often provide a variety of services, including meals, a place to sleep, and programs to help homeless people find jobs and apply for public assistance benefits. Some shelters house men only, some women only, and still others are for women and children. Very few house entire families. Pam's family had to split up to find shelter. She and her three sons live in a shelter for women and children while her husband sleeps in a men's shelter several miles away. Pam is grateful that her family has a place to stay, even though they aren't together.

As the weather becomes colder, more and more of the homeless want to sleep indoors, and lines for shelters start forming early in the afternoon. At 3:00 P.M. Arnie joins a line for shelter beds, although the shelter won't open until 5:00 P.M. He hopes that if there are no more beds by the time he reaches the front of the line, he will at least be allowed to sleep inside on the floor. Arnie is cold, temporarily sober, and ready to fight anyone who tries to take his place in line. He knows that he will not be allowed to enter a shelter if he is drunk,

A mother and her sons relax at a shelter in Denver, Colorado.

Shelters are often overcrowded and provide no privacy.

and that his place in line will make the difference between sleeping indoors and possibly freezing to death huddled in a doorway.

Many homeless people who generally live in northern cities migrate to the southern and southwestern states during the winter. These "snowbirds" strain the shelter systems in Sunbelt cities, and, as in northern cities, often there are not enough meals, beds, or services for everyone. When shelters are full, people are turned away, but sleeping on a warm street in Phoenix is preferable to sleeping on a cold street in Boston.

Those who manage to get refuge in shelters find that the living arrangements vary from one place to another. In many, there is little or no privacy, no safe place to keep personal belongings, and no guarantee that there will be a bed available on any particular night. People staying at shelters seldom get a good night's sleep

An abandoned building is this couple's home.

because they feel uncertain about the people who are sleeping nearby. The man on the corner cot could be a kind, elderly man who is down on his luck, or he could be dangerous. Nothing can be taken for granted.

Many shelters were not originally built to house people. Old armories, abandoned school buildings, and dilapidated hotels are often converted and used as shelters. Such buildings are usually in need of repair and often have no running water, no working elevators, and paint is often peeling off the walls. Some shelters are hot and steamy in the summer and bitterly cold in the winter. Cockroaches, rats, and mice are frequent nightly visitors, and hundreds of people may sleep in one large room, a situation known as warehousing. Some shelters use wire mesh to divide large rooms into individual cubicles that often resemble cages for animals rather than sleeping areas for people.

Also, many homeless people come to prefer life on the streets to the moral arrogance they encounter from workers at some shelters and charity organizations. Some people working at shelters and soup kitchens consider themselves morally as well as economically superior to the homeless people they serve, and the homeless quickly realize this. At many shelters sponsored by religious groups, homeless clients may also be required to listen to sermons and to participate in prayer sessions.

Although people who are drunk, high on drugs, or disruptive are not allowed to stay in most shelters, violence is common, and shelter life can be dangerous. "Jackrollers"—young, strong, ruthless people—are a constant threat. They wait for others to fall asleep and then steal the sleeping person's last few material possessions. The elderly are especially vulnerable to such attacks because they are less able to protect themselves.[2] In addition, shelters pose a health threat because of overcrowding, problems with personal cleanliness, and the presence of people with colds, flu, and contagious diseases such as hepatitis and tuberculosis.[3]

Sometimes homeless people refuse to stay in shelters because they feel it's degrading to be warehoused in such deplorable conditions. Tales of attacks by other shelter residents have convinced some people that their chances for survival are better on the street.

Others don't want to stay in shelters because they object to following shelter rules. For example, unless the weather is extremely cold, Arnie will not sleep in a shelter because he can't arrive drunk or take alcohol inside. On most nights Arnie would rather be drunk than warm. Other homeless people resent shelter rules such as having to be indoors by 9:00 P.M., take a shower, apply for jobs, look for housing, or help out with the chores at the shelter. Teenagers may avoid going to shelters because they're afraid of being reported as runaways and returned to the homes from which they have fled.

Rules often limit the number of nights that a person can stay at the same shelter. After reaching the limit, the homeless person must find another shelter or sleep on the street. In New York City, a group of homeless individuals, known as "mole people," sleep in subway tunnels, where they are often only inches away from live rails, which, if touched, would electrocute them. Others spend the night in phone booths or doorways. Some sleep in alleys and try to stay warm by starting fires in trash cans.

The recurring need for "three hots and a cot" drives some homeless people to commit crimes in full view of a police officer. Being sent to jail means being fed and kept warm and dry—at least for a while. Some homeless alcoholics check themselves into detoxification centers, where they can have a place to sleep indoors and have food to eat while they withdraw from alcohol. But once they return to the street they usually start drinking again.

Although many of the homeless find places to sleep at night, what do they do during the day? Dan is a 35-year-old homeless man who spends his days riding the bus or subway. For the price of the fare, Dan has a warm, relatively safe place to pass his time, and chances are that no one will realize that he is homeless. Although Arnie and some other homeless people look dirty and wear tattered clothing, Dan and many other homeless people work hard to look their best. Dan usually sleeps sitting up in order to avoid wrinkling his brown business suit.

Dan's ability to survive on the streets often depends on how well he blends into the community around him. If he fits in with the crowd, he is free to use public bathrooms and stay warm in a library or bus terminal, because he looks more like a customer than a homeless loiterer. Appearing downtrodden can mean being removed from public buildings by security guards.

Loitering in public parks and buildings has become a major issue. Most citizens believe that parks should be places for people to walk in or for children to play in, rather than campgrounds for the homeless. In Tompkins Square Park in New York City's East Village, a group of homeless people set up a shantytown that appeared to be a permanent community. An assortment of derelicts, hustlers, drug dealers, mentally ill people, and poor people forced out of gentrified apartments nearby inhabited the park. The settlement caused sanitation problems. It also led to frequent theft and the establishment of a brothel where prostitutes practiced their trade. The police tore down the shacks and tents. The squatters put them back up. The police tore them down again. The squatters put them back up again. The pattern was repeated until the park was finally closed, renovated, and replanted.[4] The park's homeless squatters were finally forced to move elsewhere.

People also want to be able to use public libraries, which their tax dollars support, without having to look at a homeless person sprawled across a table while

Some homeless people, like the man shaving in the top photo, work hard to maintain appearances and blend in with the general public. One of the squatters in New York's Tompkins Square Park (bottom) was known as "the mayor," because he kept his area clean. He lived in the park for seven years—with about 150 other homeless people.

Police in riot gear evicted almost 200 people from Tompkins Square Park in 1991.

taking a nap. They want to be able to shop downtown without being hassled by panhandlers asking for a handout, and they want to sit in the lobby of a museum without enduring the wretched smell of a person living on the street. Continual encounters in public places like these often lessen the compassion the general public has for the homeless.

But if homeless people are not allowed to stay in public places, where can they go during the day? Some cities have day-shelter programs where homeless people are offered hot showers, clean clothing, a storage area where possessions may be safely kept for a day or more, and the use of a telephone to make calls about jobs and housing. Homeless people are often allowed to use the address of day shelters as their mailing address. This enables them to have food stamps and welfare checks

mailed to them. Many day shelters offer additional services such as programs to help the mentally ill, housing
and job counseling, and drug and alcohol rehabilitation
programs.

Some homeless people have full-time or part-time jobs.
Others wait in line hoping for one-day work assignments.
Other homeless people collect discarded soda pop and
beer cans to redeem at a recycling center. Hundreds of
dollars a month can be earned by "doing the cans."[5] In
spite of their efforts to work, however, homeless people
seldom earn enough money to support themselves.

Panhandling is another way homeless people get
money, and the practice takes place on streets throughout the United States. Panhandlers hold signs that say,
"Will work for food," but many don't really want to work.
They're looking for a handout, and on a good day they
can make more money standing on a corner than by
working for eight hours at a minimum-wage job.

This family lives in a single room of a shelter that used to be a hotel. Beds are shared, and there is little space for play.

HOMELESS CHILDREN AND THEIR FAMILIES

"Shelter boy, shelter boy! Peter is a shelter boy!" As the circle of voices surrounded him, Peter clenched his fists and closed his eyes. When his teacher approached with a scowl on her face, the crowd of children vanished, leaving Peter alone once more.

According to Esther S. Merves of the Department of Sociology at Kenyon College, the national "rate of poverty in 1984 for female-headed families was 34.5 percent, five times the rate for all other families. In female-headed families of black and Spanish origin, the poverty rates were 51.7 percent and 53.4 percent, respectively. The impact of these rates is seen clearly in the dramatic child poverty rate: 16 percent of all white children, 39 percent of all children of Spanish origin, and 46 percent of all black children are poor."[1] Many of these families are homeless or at risk of becoming homeless. Jonathan Kozol, author of *Rachel and Her Children,* writes that almost 500,000 American children were homeless in 1988—although most of them didn't live on the street.[2] Many are in foster care or are in families that are doubled up with friends or relatives. Some, like Peter, live in shelters.

Young children have become the fastest-growing group of homeless people in the United States.[3] For some children, problems associated with homelessness begin even before they are born. Because of medical costs and the difficulty of getting to a doctor, many homeless pregnant women do not receive adequate prenatal care. These women are three times more likely to have low birth-weight babies.[4] Such children have a lower survival rate than other babies and are nine times more likely to have brain disorders or nervous-system impairments.[5]

Healthy babies are also affected by homelessness, because they need diapers, clothing, toys, and plenty of sleep and attention. Homeless mothers may be forced to substitute folded newspapers for diapers.[6] Commercially produced baby formula, made by mixing measured amounts of water and powder, is often a newborn baby's only food. When mixed properly, it makes a nutritious, milklike drink, but many extremely poor mothers add extra water to the mixture to make a little extra formula. Although this diluted mixture may fill a baby's stomach, the child isn't getting proper nourishment. Some homeless mothers even feed their babies nondairy coffee creamer, which provides no nourishment at all.[7] Also, homeless mothers usually don't have access to stoves or refrigerators to warm and store baby formula or other food.

During the first years of life, a baby's brain develops quickly. If it doesn't develop properly during this time, chances are the child may never be mentally and emotionally normal. Drinking diluted baby formula can cause

Shelters and soup kitchens do not usually serve the sort of food that very young children need for healthy growth and development.

irreversible brain damage to children. They may develop slowly, walking later than other children and not learning as quickly or as much as others.

As babies get older, they need solid food, but they aren't able to eat the same food that older children and adults eat. Providing homeless infants with nourishing food is difficult because the prepared baby food for sale in supermarkets is expensive, and soup kitchens usually prepare food appropriate only for adults. As with diluted formula, eating a diet lacking proper nutrition can cause brain damage in children.

Homeless children have little opportunity for play and few toys to play with. The only nap a homeless toddler might get is in a bus station or on a park bench. Homeless children may wear an outfit until it is bursting at

While staying in a shelter, this woman takes advantage of the opportunity to wash clothes.

the seams because it's the only outfit they have, or they may be draped in oversize hand-me-downs. Without a place to wash their clothes or themselves, homeless children are often dirty. Sometimes, because of overflowing sewage in the bathrooms of their temporary housing units, they are extremely dirty.

Just going to the bathroom can be an ordeal for homeless children, who often face a walk of several blocks to reach the nearest building that has a public restroom. When a mother and her young children arrive, they may be told to leave—that they are not welcome there. Without a toilet available, the homeless relieve themselves wherever they can, perhaps in a nearby alley or behind a tree, usually without privacy. Toilet training a toddler under such conditions is almost impossible.

Poor health is also a reality for many homeless children. Peggy McIntire, director of Cuidando Los Niños, a day-care center for homeless children in Albuquerque, New Mexico, says, "They face continually being sick. They have more ear infections. They have more strep throat. They have more respiratory illnesses than housed kids. They have a lot of problems with bladder infections and kidney infections because they cannot bathe."[8]

Once homeless children get sick, they have a difficult time getting well again. For example, when Juan got strep throat, a doctor gave his mother some medicine for Juan to take three times a day for 10 days. However, the medicine must be refrigerated, and Juan's mother doesn't have a refrigerator—or even a teaspoon to measure

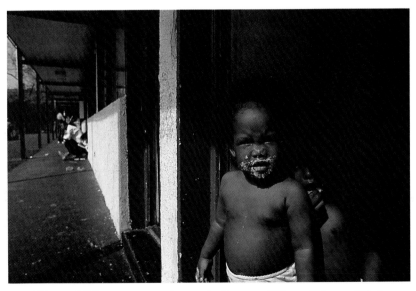

These children are growing up in the squalid conditions of their family's temporary housing.

Homeless children have nowhere to rest when they're sick, they have few toys to play with, and they sometimes have to walk long distances to use public bathrooms.

the exact dosage. And how will Juan get the rest he needs when he has no bed?

McIntire believes that "Each child is entitled to one joyful experience a day. Our kids are real lucky to have maybe one a year, or one a lifetime. These are serious kids." She describes homeless one to five-year-olds who come to the day-care center without shoes, socks, coats, and sometimes without underwear. These homeless preschoolers seldom laugh. If they have shoes, they sleep with them on, because they're worried that their shoes will be stolen if they take them off. They cling to toys

Going to school can be stressful for homeless children.

so no one will snatch them away. Yet the 26 children who are enrolled at Cuidando Los Niños day-care center are fortunate. During the day they are fed, loved, and kept warm. Unfortunately, only a handful of day-care programs for homeless children exist.

Homeless school-age children face their own set of problems. School is often a stressful, unsuccessful experience for them, and they are sometimes the targets of ridicule. Peter, for example, frequently comes to school tired and without having eaten breakfast. His homework is seldom done because shelters offer few places in which to study, and he has no school supplies to work with. During school, Peter is usually too worried about where he will be staying that night to concentrate fully on his schoolwork.

Truancy is a common problem among homeless children, who tend to change schools frequently, as they move from one living arrangement to another.

Many homeless children are two to three years behind their classmates in their schoolwork, and they may never catch up.[9] Some homeless children, like Peter, cope with school failure by withdrawing into themselves and trying to make themselves invisible. Other children have behavior problems.

Just when Peter finally settles into a school, his family may move to another shelter. This means either that Peter must start all over again in a new school, or that special arrangements must be made so Peter can continue to attend his present school. Many homeless children would rather spend several hours a day riding public transportation to and from school than start all over again in an unfamiliar setting.

Although the law requires all children between the ages of 5 and 16 to attend school, not all homeless children do so. A study done by the U.S. Conference of Mayors found that 43 percent of homeless children in the United States do not attend school.[10] Pam's son Robby should be in first grade, but he's missed half the school year. Pam does her best to help Robby and her two other sons, but she, too, is under a great deal of stress dealing with her own problems. She said, "I feel mad that I can't do better, and I feel sad too."

Because their own needs are so great, many homeless parents are not able to nurture their children or provide them with emotional support and stability. When parents are considered unable to care for their children, a social worker from a welfare agency might investigate the situation to determine whether the child is being abused or neglected. In some states, parents may be considered guilty of neglect if they fail to provide their

Many homeless families choose to live in makeshift housing rather than in shelters, because they fear their children will be taken away from them if their situation is reported to authorities.

children with a minimal level of shelter, food, and clothing.[11] If social workers determine that neglect or abuse is occurring, they or the police have the authority to remove children from their present living situation and place them in emergency shelter facilities. Sometimes children are transferred to the care of a willing relative or placed in foster homes, where they are fed, clothed, and housed until their parents are able to care for them again.

To keep their families together, many homeless parents will not apply for public assistance benefits or sleep in shelters. They are afraid that if their family's situation is known, they will be reported to the authorities, and their children will be taken away. Without shelter, food stamps, or support from other public assistance programs, families have a difficult time surviving.

What do homeless children need? McIntire believes that "these little children need time to grow and experience the things that kids [who live] in houses experience. They need to have some kind of success." But homelessness, by its very nature, is not a lifestyle built on success. Homelessness is often a matter of moving one step forward and two steps back.

Imagine a game called "Homelessness." The object of the game is for you and your family to find your way out of homelessness. A roll of the dice, some unlucky breaks or personal tragedy, and you and your family become players. You roll a two with the dice and move your playing piece forward. You land on the "Apply for Benefits" square. Your family is eligible to receive benefits from government public assistance programs. Move forward one space. Hope is in sight! But now you must fill out the proper paperwork. If you are educated and speak English, you might be able to fill out the forms yourself. If not, you and your family have to move backward on the game board until you can find somebody to help you. As you are filling out the paperwork, you are asked, "Where should your food stamps and welfare checks be sent?" No address? No benefits. Return to square one. Once you have found an address where benefits can be mailed, and if your application for benefits is accepted, you may move forward two spaces as long as budget cutbacks and changes in program regulations don't push you back again.

This family often depends on soup kitchens for food.

You roll a three and land on the "Apply for a Job" space. After several days of reading the newspaper and making phone calls, you have a chance to apply for a job. You can move forward five additional spaces if you make a good impression at the job interview. What will you wear? Certainly not those tattered clothes on your back. Go back two spaces. And you can't very well drag your children along for the interview. There's nobody to watch them? Tough break, back another space. Even if you make it to the interview, do you have the education and skills an employer wants? Where can the employer reach you later to let you know you've gotten the job? No telephone or address? You sound like a homeless person to an employer, and that makes you an employment risk—someone the employer probably can't rely on. The job is given to someone else. Move back another two spaces.

Without a job, it's almost impossible for you to ever reach the other parts of the game board, such as "Getting off the Streets," "Feeding and Clothing Your Family," or "Finding a Home." For many players the game is over.

It's your lucky day. You roll a six, which means you got a job! You're one of the fortunate homeless people that is able to move past the "Apply for a Job" space onto the "Working for a Living" space. At last a steady income! Move forward five spaces. But a few weeks later the school calls to notify you that your daughter has the flu. You have to leave work and take two days off to care for her. Go back one space. The flu is contagious. Your son gets it next, and then you get it too. After a week of absences, you no longer have a job.

This woman and her children were evicted from their one-bedroom apartment in Miami Beach, Florida, where they had slept on a rusty double bed and two mattresses spread on the floor.

If the game of "Homelessness" doesn't seem like much fun, imagine trying to live it. There are few successes, and even fewer winners. Instead many homeless families spend months or even years moving forward and back, forward and back, forward and back....

Unless circumstances change for his family, Peter will remain a "shelter boy." The longer Peter is homeless, the less chance he has of ever getting out of the cycle of poverty and homelessness. Instead of learning to read and write, Peter will learn the entrenched culture of dependence and hopelessness. Peter may eventually become a "shelter man" with shelter children of his own.

These teens are living on the street in Phoenix, Arizona.

HOMELESS OR HOPELESS?

"Me personally, I was brought up with drugs in my house. It was all around me and my parents introduced me to drugs.... We used to do drugs together sometimes," explains James, sitting on a stool in the kitchen of a shelter for runaway youths. "After a while I started to get into drugs real heavily. I just went down the tubes from there. I didn't want to stay at home anymore because I couldn't do all the different drugs I wanted to.... My mom, she would let me drink but she didn't want to see me drunk all the time and that's the way I wanted to be because that's the way I wanted to cope with my depression. I thought it made me feel better. So I didn't want to be at home no more. I just went out on the streets."[1]

James left home when he was 15. He doubled up with friends and dropped out of high school. In order to support his drug habit, James sold drugs for a local dealer and stole cars. Eventually the police caught him, and he was sent to a home for delinquent youths. Because James had been in trouble with the law and because his mother

Many taxpayers think that the government should not spend money to support able-bodied people who could take care of themselves if they wanted to work.

had problems of her own, she didn't want him to come back home. James states, "The reality hit me...that nobody was there for me. I was on my own."

James was transferred to a shelter for teenagers for two months. He went back to high school, but when he was sent to another shelter, he had to start over at a different high school. "At first, things were going pretty well," James explains. "But I got back into the bad people at school, started hanging around with them. And then I went back into my drugs, back into my running around and stuff."

James felt depressed after being sent to a detention home again after stealing another car—so depressed that he didn't want to live. An evaluation by a psychiatrist showed that James was suffering from extreme depression, and he was admitted to a mental health center. For almost a year, James took prescribed medication, and a counselor helped him deal with his problems. During this same time, his stepfather committed suicide after getting drunk and beating James's mother. After that, James explains, "I just decided. The example of what drinking did with him...I figured it was up to me. I had to do it alone."

Many people would agree with James. They believe that "the responsibility of caring for oneself lies with the individual."[2] Intolerance toward the homeless has increased as more Americans view welfare programs as catering to people who could work if they wanted to. Those who seem to have brought on their own problems—those who have drug or alcohol problems, those who have quit their jobs, or those who are restless and just don't want to work on a regular basis—draw the same unsympathetic response. For example, Jake, a 30-year-old blond woman with tatoos decorating her chest lies back in a bed of blankets and heavy-metal cassette tapes in front of City Hall in San Francisco. Her two companions, Red, 29, and Gadget, 24, are next to her. Jake says, "I see this as a form of anarchy. We're not going to hide somewhere. Just us being here is a protest." When pressed about why they don't go out and get jobs, Gadget responds, "I'm not going to go flip burgers at some McDonald's so I can share a tiny apartment with a bunch of crazy [people]."[3]

Many people reason that homeless people like Jake have made their own choices and must face the consequences. They do not believe that it is the responsibility

These young people have chosen an alternative lifestyle on the street.

A homeless man naps beside a scenic California harbor.

of taxpayers to support federal assistance programs for people who could take care of themselves. As he left office in 1988, former president Ronald Reagan repeated his personal view on homelessness—that is, that the homeless are on the streets by choice and prefer this to the available shelters, that "a large proportion" of them have mental problems, and that the jobless are simply not motivated.[4]

Some people applaud budget cuts to welfare programs because they believe that too much money is wasted on government assistance programs that make poor people dependent on welfare.[5] They insist that people who receive public assistance have little incentive to become productive members of society. Welfare programs, they maintain, often become a way of life for the long-term

Some people argue that providing housing and welfare programs encourages a sense of dependency that gets passed on from one generation to another. This couple has no home and little food. Neither of them has a job. Will their child also be a welfare recipient when she grows up?

poor, and poverty becomes cyclical. Their parents lived on welfare, they live on welfare, and their children probably will as well. In a *Fortune* article, Myron Magnet talks about the "hydralike" quality of some social problems, "growing worse and more intractable as a result of the efforts made to solve them." Magnet continues, "The underclass's entrenched culture of dependence, its inability from one generation to another to participate in the larger society, the stunted development of its human potentialities—all this was fostered by the welfare system and the War on Poverty [a program developed during President Lyndon Johnson's administration]."[6]

C. Brandon Crocker also presents a strong case for the idea that individuals are ultimately responsible for

For this man, dinner will consist of whatever bits of food he can find in dumpsters. He carries his bed and personal articles on his back.

themselves, and he argues that shelter staffs should make this point clear. He writes, "If those working with the homeless don't expect the population with which they deal to better their circumstances through their own diligence, the homeless will develop the same attitude"—one of psychological dependence.[7]

Some observers believe that if government funding were reduced, individuals and families who cheat and abuse the welfare system would be cut from programs. Assistance, they explain, would then be available only for those who are most in need of help. Other people would like to reduce or completely eliminate the federal government's role in welfare programs. This group wants to transfer the responsibility for the poor and the homeless to local and state governments and to private agencies. Because the problems of extreme poverty and homelessness vary so much throughout the United States, these individuals believe that programs will be effective only if they are developed, funded, and monitored at the state or community level.[8]

Many people have lost their sympathy for the homeless after panhandlers have aggressively and repeatedly asked them for money in city streets and parks. Most concerned citizens don't want their neighborhood parks turned into shantytowns and sandboxes turned into urinals. In some city parks, homeless individuals jam into public bathroom stalls to sleep, and they sometimes charge 50 cents to move their bedding before anyone else can enter.[9] Such behavior has led some cities to enact ordinances that prohibit panhandling and sleeping in public places.[10] Some cities have even declared that garbage in trash bins is public property, thereby

The sign on this vacant building warns homeless people that might be scavenging for food. It says, "In This Area Do Not Pick Up Any Bags, Boxes, or Trays; They May Contain Poison Food."

making it illegal for people to forage in dumpsters. In Fort Lauderdale, Florida, a city councilman suggested spraying the trash in dumpsters with rat poison to discourage homeless people from foraging. The way to "get rid of vermin," he observed, is to cut their food supply.[11] Grocers in Santa Barbara, California, sprinkled bleach on the food discarded in their dumpsters.[12] The city of Laramie, Wyoming, provides homeless people with shelter for one night. "On the next morning, an organization called 'The Good Samaritan Fund' gives them one-way tickets to another town."[13] These rather drastic responses to homelessness are indicative of what Mayor Loni Hancock of Berkeley, California, refers to as "compassion fatigue." This hard-line attitude is being assumed

In hopes of getting a bed for the night, these men (top) begin to form a line in front of a shelter in Denver, Colorado. A group of AFDC (Aid to Families with Dependent Children) mothers gather to chat (bottom).

by a growing number of Americans whose sympathy is waning after decades of widespread and visible homelessness that seems to have no end.[14]

Many people believe that funding emergency programs for the homeless is like putting pans under a leaky ceiling. It is a stopgap measure, but the problem won't end until the ceiling is fixed. Instead of funding programs to help the homeless, they say, we should be funneling our money and energy into improving American technology and our trade balance. Such measures, in the end, will be the best help for the homeless because they will contribute to a strong economy, which this group believes would lead to more jobs and less homelessness.

Furthermore, the federal government already spends massive amounts of money on health and human services. To assist the extremely poor and to keep them from falling into homelessness, the federal government developed programs and services to provide a "safety net." These programs and services assist with basic needs for food, housing, income, and medical care. Most poor people receive assistance through Medicaid, Aid to Families with Dependent Children (AFDC), Supplemental Security Income for the Aged, Blind, and Disabled (SSI), and the Food Stamp Program. Women, Infants, and Children (WIC) provides allotments for nutritional supplements for pregnant women and children under five. In addition, many states also have a General Assistance (GA) program, which is an income support program that helps unattached persons—those who are unmarried and without children. Among the states that provide GA, however, none provides payments that reach $4,000 a year, less than the poverty line for individuals. Some

🏠 Aid to Families with Dependent Children is a federal program that provides income for children and their families or guardians.

🏠 The Food Stamp Program helps low-income persons buy more and better food than they could otherwise afford. Each household receives a certain number of coupons called food stamps. When recipients are checking out at the supermarket, they give the food stamps to the cashier to pay for their groceries.

🏠 Medicaid provides free medical care to the needy. Services include appointments with doctors, hospital treatment, and nursing-home care. Medicaid also pays for eyeglasses, prescription drugs, hearing aids, and other medical items.

• •

states, such as Texas, Alabama, and Tennessee, have no income support programs for this segment of the population.[15]

Many people believe that cutbacks and restrictions in federal programs such as food stamps and AFDC have left gaping holes in the safety net for the extremely poor. As a result, they say, thousands of America's poorest people have fallen through the safety net and landed in extreme poverty and homelessness. They want to see more federal involvement and increased funding for public assistance programs.

Crocker replies that "most of the chronically homeless—the mentally ill and those who have withdrawn from society through the use of drugs and alcohol—are not a group of people who fell through 'holes' in the safety net—they jumped off the safety net."[16]

⌂ Supplemental Security Income provides financial aid to needy people who are at least 65 years old, blind, or disabled.

⌂ Women, Infants, and Children is a major weapon in preventing infant death, but the program reaches only about one-third of those who need it nationwide.

• • • • • • • • • •

⌂ Some families receive benefits from more than one welfare program. For example, a mother who is receiving AFDC funds would probably also receive food stamps and Medicaid coverage. In 1989 many families couldn't make ends meet, even with benefits from two or more public assistance programs.

• •

Is he correct? Marsha McMurray-Avila, executive director of the Health Care for the Homeless program in Albuquerque, New Mexico, and a board member of the National Coalition for the Homeless, doesn't think so. She believes that society must respond to the problem of homelessness at three different levels: the emergency level, which includes shelters, meal programs, and medical care; a service level to stabilize the lives of the homeless and get them back into the mainstream; and a third level of preventive programs to keep people from becoming homeless.[17]

In many cities, shelters are one of the few services available to homeless people, but there aren't enough of them, according to McMurray-Avila. In 1989 the city of Chicago had a homeless population estimated at 40,000 people, but there were only 2,800 to 3,200 shelter beds

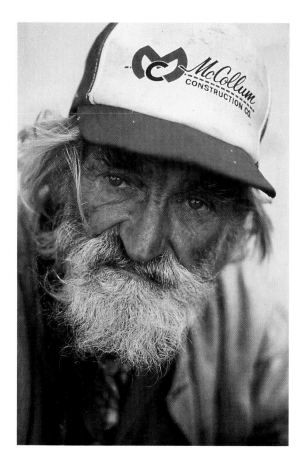

Lack of housing is only one of the problems that plagues homeless Americans. They also lack adequate nutrition and medical care.

available.[18] Such shortages are common throughout the country.

The health problems of the homeless also seem overwhelming. Lillian Gelberg of the University of California reported that two-thirds of the homeless people she interviewed had physical problems that required immediate medical attention. About one-third were underweight or malnourished, and half of them suffered from chronic illnesses.[19]

Medical care is costly, and homeless people seldom have health insurance. Therefore, many homeless people wait in long lines for treatment at hospital clinics, while others ignore their health problems until they are severe and need emergency treatment. Medicaid helps many poor and homeless people pay their medical expenses, but some states have such strict eligibility requirements that homeless people may not qualify for assistance. Other homeless people do not receive Medicaid benefits because they don't know they are eligible, or they don't know how to apply for them.

What can be done to ensure that homeless Americans have adequate medical care? Developing education and outreach programs to inform homeless people about public assistance benefits is a first step, according to some homeless advocates. In addition, they recommend

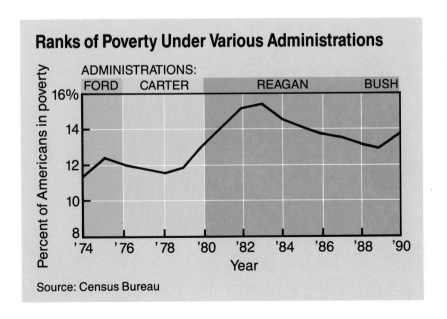

that existing health care programs for the homeless be expanded and adequately funded. However, members of the NCH believe that meeting the medical needs of the poor and homeless is such a huge task that a national health policy is necessary. According to the NCH, one part of such a policy might be a health insurance plan to guarantee health care to any American, even those who are unable to pay.[20] Such a program would help the 37 million Americans who are medically uninsured.[21] It would also be extraordinarily costly.

Alternative ways of meeting the health care needs of homeless people are being explored. One innovative program called Project Street Beat helps hundreds of teen-

A child receives a free checkup at a clinic in a family shelter in Denver, Colorado.

agers living on the streets of New York City. Instead of waiting until homeless teenagers come into clinics for help, vans with medical equipment and trained personnel drive around areas in which homeless teens live. The staff offers them emotional support as well as free medical care, warm meals, and clean clothes.[22]

Although such programs that address the immediate needs of the homeless are important, the NCH insists that "emergency shelters and food assistance are only first steps in a more comprehensive solution to the problem of homelessness."[23] Advocates for the homeless think that the second level of response to homelessness involves transitional shelter programs—services that help homeless people get off the street, stabilize their lives, and get back into the community. Such programs might include substance abuse rehabilitation, professional help for the mentally ill, and opportunities for education and job training.

Several cities already offer transitional shelter programs to homeless families, runaway teenagers, or people with substance abuse problems. These programs go beyond the traditional shelter idea of merely warehousing the homeless. The New England Shelter for Homeless Veterans in Boston, for example, offers U.S. veterans services such as alcohol and drug treatment programs, job counseling, stress therapy, and housing referrals.[24] Washington House in Philadelphia works specifically with homeless substance abusers. Homeless men stay at this facility for up to six months while they recover from their drug or alcohol addictions. The center also provides support services such as job counseling, Alcoholics Anonymous, and Narcotics Anonymous.[25]

Appropriate aftercare is a major part of successfully rehabilitating homeless alcohol and drug abusers. In his book *Address Unknown: The Homeless in America,* James D. Wright states that "the best treatment and rehabilitation facilities imaginable can have but modest effects if, at the end of treatment, the patient returns to a life on the streets, which has been the typical case."[26] He recommends creating transitional alcohol-free hotels where homeless people can live with and be supported by others who are trying to stay free of drugs and alcohol.

Homeless people often need job training and education programs to get back on their feet. As part of the Ready, Willing, and Able program in New York City, homeless men and women earn five dollars an hour while they learn the basics of construction work. During the nine-month training period, crews replace torn-down walls, paint, put in flooring, and do other renovation work on buildings that will be used by homeless families. Through a referral service, the city helps place graduates in permanent jobs.[27] Many other cities also have programs to help the homeless develop job skills.

Homeless people who are mentally ill require special services that address their particular needs. New York City has several privately run shelters for the mentally ill homeless, including the Bridge, Community Access, and the St. Francis Residence programs. Volunteers and psychiatric professionals make sure that mentally ill clients take their medication, wash themselves, eat nourishing food, and generally know how to care for themselves.[28]

Other programs, such as New Mexico's Project Care and Health Care for the Homeless, provide case man-

***Very few shelters provide job training or follow-up services for
homeless people.***

agement services. Case managers are assigned to mentally ill clients to help them find transitional housing,
apply for public assistance benefits, learn to budget
their money, and arrange for psychiatric evaluation and
proper medication. They also help the mentally ill develop basic life skills such as how to cook, shop, and
dress properly.[29] Such programs, however, are in short
supply and are therefore unavailable to most of the
homeless people who need them.

Other health care programs try to connect homeless
people with medical resources. As of 1990, the United
States had 112 Health Care for the Homeless programs
that offered services such as free medical and dental
care, eye examinations, and hearing tests. Health Care
for the Homeless also helps people find places to live and

Without rehabilitation programs such as the one run by the Salvation Army in Canoga Park, California (above), homeless substance abusers end up back on the street.

offers support services such as substance abuse and mental health programs.[30]

What is the difference between homeless people who eventually rejoin the community and the large minority of individuals who remain homeless? Marsha McMurray-Avila explains: "It's a combination of two things happening at the same time—the motivation in a person to change combined with...an opportunity to do so. Very often what happens is those two things don't meet. You may have the opportunity available and the person's not ready. Or [more often] you've got a person who's ready ...and there's no resources for him to plug into."

James is a good example. He was homeless for three years, but due to a combination of existing services and his own motivation, he was able to change his life. James is now 20, he no longer uses drugs or alcohol, and he has earned his high school equivalency degree. James shares his life story with younger children through the Teens against Drugs program and encourages them to stay away from drugs. He credits his success to the support of people and programs that were available when he needed them. Where would he be today without them? James states frankly, "I can say right now that I wouldn't be alive, I'd be dead...if I was still living with my friends doing those same drugs." McMurray-Avila believes that if all homeless people are to have access to resources that might get them off the street, a strong network of transitional level programs needs to be developed and funded.

Advocates for the homeless also want preventive programs—those that keep people from becoming homeless. They see this as the third level of response to homeless-

Just evicted from their apartment, this family sits on a mattress surrounded by other pieces of furniture and clothing.

ness and the one most often ignored. McMurray-Avila points out, "It is hard to stop responding to the emergency, but unless we can...get that long-term view, we'll burn ourselves out....We have to stop...the root problem." She feels that it is necessary to find the source of the problem—to identify the reasons that people become homeless—and then develop programs to prevent homelessness.

Some states have explored ways to prevent people from losing their homes. New Jersey, for example, has implemented a program to help needy people with overdue rent payments. In one year alone, this program helped 8,000 people stay in their homes.[31] Other states have tenant mediation programs to help landlords and tenants resolve issues that might lead to eviction and possible homelessness.

Author James D. Wright supports the implementation of a national rent insurance program as a way to prevent homelessness. He cites research indicating that most homeless people follow a pattern of occasional homelessness followed by periods of living in conventional housing. These "episodically homeless" are affected by the economy, loss of jobs, and the availability of low-income housing. Wright suggests that "for a nominal sum, a family or single individual could protect against the short-term loss of income that...can cause a consequent loss of housing."[32] He proposes that people living close to the poverty line and those who spend 40 percent or more of their income for housing might be eligible for such a federally subsidized program. Wright believes that overall, it is more cost-effective to offer peo-

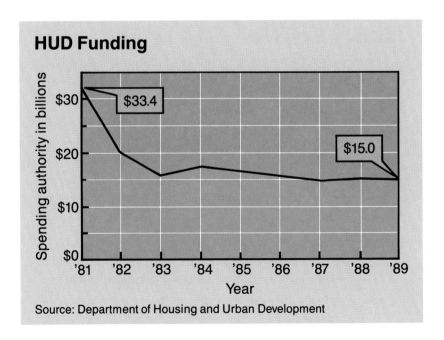

HUD Funding

Spending authority in billions

$33.4

$15.0

Year

Source: Department of Housing and Urban Development

ple help when they need it, through a rent insurance plan, than to care for them after they become homeless.

The NCH and other advocacy groups believe that an adequate supply of low-income housing—including renovated buildings as well as newly constructed ones—is the key to preventing homelessness. Housing advocates would like existing low-income housing units to be maintained rather than destroyed or gentrified, and some cities have been successful in rehabilitating such units. In New York, for instance, more than 12,500 low-income apartments have been restored since 1983.[33]

Another New York success story resulted from a joint effort of the private sector and government agencies. The partnership acquires buildings from owners who have not paid their taxes. It then renovates the properties and converts them into low-income housing units. Although the program is projected to cost $5.1 billion over 10 years, New York expects to gain over 250,000 low-income units that can be used by the homeless.[34] To meet the growing demand for low-income housing, however, new dwellings must also be built.[35] Wright has proposed building boardinghouses with on-site medical and mental health care.[36] After studying the problem of homelessness, Jonathan Kozol concluded that "only a multi-billion-dollar federal program can create the millions of new units that are needed, and only a sense of national emergency can render allocations on this scale politically conceivable."[37]

Many advocates for the homeless believe that legislation should be passed to ensure the right to shelter. Some, like Jonathan Kozol, have even suggested that a national policy be established to provide relief to the

A cardboard box provides shelter for this man. Only his shoes can be seen among the blankets.

Thousands of people attended the Housing Now! march in 1989.

homeless.[38] On October 7, 1989, more than 250,000 people came together in Washington, D.C., for the Housing Now! march. From across the country, religious leaders joined unemployed workers, homeless people, and concerned citizens to demand that housing be made a priority. In response, Representative Floyd Flake introduced legislation (H.R. 4621) in Congress to authorize spending $125 billion over five years and to develop an array of programs designed to provide four million additional subsidized housing units.[39] The NCH viewed this bill as an important milestone because it provided the first and only comprehensive housing program for the nation's homeless and for those at risk of becoming homeless. Although the NCH knew that because of tight budget constraints Congress would never pass the bill, they hoped that it would inspire serious discussion of the issues and grassroots efforts to provide housing.[40]

Nothing in our constitution states that shelter is an inalienable right, and not everyone believes that the homeless have a right to shelter. But Professor Gregg Barak of the University of Alabama points out that the rights of the homeless seem to be established in the minds of many Americans.[41] Based on this idea, public interest lawyers in New York sued the city in the 1979 case *Callahan v. Carey.* They claimed that New York had an obligation to provide shelter for homeless men, and the New York Supreme Court agreed.[42]

Such rights, however, are not established in the minds of many other Americans. In 1990 the city council of Washington, D.C., voted to cut $19 million from the budget for homelessness, and it questioned whether the city was required to provide shelter for all those in

Changes over a 3-Year Period in the Rental Housing of Selected Metro Areas*

	Old units removed (number)	Median rent	New units built (number)	Median rent
All 60 cities	322,700		203,300	
Specific cities				
Boston (1974–77)	6,300	$141	2,600	$212
Chicago (1975–78)	33,700	145	4,300	253
Cleveland (1976–79)	6,900	124	500	185
Detroit (1974–77)	13,600	109	2,800	131
New York (1976–79)	92,400	160	27,800	258
Newark (1974–77)	7,200	141	1,200	213
Philadelphia (1975–78)	8,900	115	3,000	302
St. Louis (1976–79)	7,900	103	400	130
San Francisco (1975–78)	5,900	82	2,600	281
Washington, DC (1974–77)	6,100	126	1,500	294

* The information presented in this table comes from the Annual Housing Survey conducted by the US Census Bureau, which surveys one-third of its total sample of 60 SMAs each year, so that the complete cycle takes 3 years. Thus, the figures above represent three different 3-year periods: for some cities it was 1974–1977; for others it was 1975–1978; for still others it was 1976–1979.

need—contrary to Initiative 17, the Right to Shelter Act they had passed in 1984.[43] In that same year, Philadelphia cut $2 million from a shelter program for the homeless.[44]

Many people believe that a guaranteed right to shelter would increase the number of people who expect the government to provide shelter, thus adding to the total cost of any housing program. Authors Charles Hoch and Robert Slayton believe that shelters actually promote dependency. They write, "Ultimately, the shelter system does little to reduce either the sources of homelessness or equip the homeless to achieve independence."[45]

Other shelter critics argue that housing isn't the basic problem. They point out that many homeless people have medical, mental, and substance abuse problems and are thus incapable of functioning in society even when they are housed or sheltered. They also believe that many of the unemployed could find jobs and support themselves if they wanted to work. They hesitate to support legislation that addresses a right to shelter without first dealing with what they perceive as the underlying causes of homelessness.

In order to be effective, legislation must first be passed, then fully funded and enforced. Congress and other legislative bodies can pass a bill, but if money is not appropriated (set aside) for its enforcement, the bill will have little or no effect. A case in point is the 1987 Stewart B. McKinney Homeless Assistance Act. Congress passed the legislation, which authorized $1 billion for job training programs, emergency and transitional shelters, and other services to help the homeless. However, only $7 million of the authorized funds were actually approved for expenditure. Therefore, this legislation did not have the impact on homelessness that most advocates had hoped for.[46]

Advocates for the homeless believe that to make the elimination of homelessness a national priority, Americans must acknowledge the severity of the problem and make a commitment to solve it. Even those opposed to spending federal funds want the problem addressed in some way. Solutions may require merging several approaches and points of view as well as answering some important questions. Are homeless people deserving of sympathy and support? Are we, as a society, responsible for caring for the needs of the homeless? Are citizens and lawmakers willing to allocate the billions of dollars experts believe it will take to adequately respond to homelessness at the emergency, transitional, and preventive levels? Instead of just financially supporting programs such as community-based residences for the mentally ill and low-income public housing, are citizens willing to have such facilities in their own neighborhoods? The answers to these and other questions may determine whether the situation of the homeless in the United States is hopeless or not.

This family lives in an abandoned building—viewed through shattered glass.

PIECES OF THE PUZZLE

Depending upon which study is used, between 250,000 and 3 million Americans are currently homeless. Some experts estimate that another 27 million people are one paycheck away from losing their homes, and their future is bleak.[1] According to a study funded by the U.S. Congress, as many as 19 million Americans may be homeless by the year 2003 unless action is taken now.[2]

But who, if anyone, is responsible for taking care of the homeless? Many people hold the homeless responsible for their plight. Others believe that the federal government should address the problem, but the government is seriously in debt. Money is scarce even for existing programs, and the idea of paying for new programs is not a popular one. Currently, the United States spends more money each year than it takes in, creating an enormous deficit. Some people argue that because of this deficit, money is simply not available to fund housing and other welfare programs.

Most state and local governments lack the money and other resources necessary to respond to homelessness in any significant way. Local governments often count on the charity of private groups, businesses, and caring individuals to help the homeless. But private efforts alone cannot solve the problem.

Sometimes individual efforts do make a difference, however. When Trevor Ferrell was 11, he watched a TV program about people living on the streets of nearby Philadelphia. Wanting to see homelessness for himself, Trevor asked his parents to drive him into the city. Trevor gave away his blanket to a homeless person, but he wanted to do more. He talked with neighbors and wrote notices asking for more blankets. When word got out about Trevor's concern for the homeless, churches, community groups, and volunteers caught his spirit of caring and wanted to help. Now there are thousands of people involved in "Trevor's Campaign." Volunteers prepare and serve meals to the homeless and donate various items to people in need. A 33-room hotel in downtown Philadelphia has been renovated and is now "Trevor's Place," a shelter for homeless mothers with small children.[3]

Trevor is not alone in his efforts. Michael Greenberg learned the joy of giving from his father. During the Great Depression of the 1930s, his father would often put an extra sandwich or a coffee cake into the bags of his bakery shop customers, even though he and his family had very little money. Michael Greenberg also knew what it was like to have cold hands. One day he lost a glove while carrying supplies into the bakery. Since money was so limited, he was ashamed to ask for new gloves and spent the winter with one gloveless hand. After his father died, Greenberg looked for a way to honor him. In tribute to his father, Greenberg decided

***Private charities operate many shelters for the homeless, such
as the one above.***

to give gloves to people living on the street in Manhattan's Bowery area. He started more than 25 years ago by purchasing 72 pairs of gloves and giving them away. When others heard of his efforts, they wanted to get involved. Today the "glove man" receives gloves from around the world to distribute to the homeless.[4]

For 17 years Mitch Snyder was an advocate for the homeless. In the 1980s, he built a shack city—called Reaganville—in front of the White House. He also rallied developers to refurbish abandoned buildings and urged food companies to give their surplus fruits and vegetables to soup kitchens.[5] In 1984 Snyder went on a 51-day hunger strike in an attempt to persuade the federal government to turn an abandoned building into a model shelter for the homeless. Federal City Shelter,

When Trevor Ferrell, right, was 11, he began a campaign against homelessness in Philadelphia, Pennsylvania.

which offers food, clothing, education programs, and shelter to more than 2,000 people each day, was the result of his efforts.

Bill Moss didn't set out to solve the country's homeless problem. He just wanted to do what he could to keep homeless people from freezing. Moss designed an inexpensive, portable instant shelter for homeless people. The street tent, which costs about $49, is made of cardboard, packs flat, and opens in minutes to provide a small, temporary shelter for a homeless individual.[6]

Hutchinson Persons, a rock musician, decided to help the homeless by providing them with a way to raise money. Instead of panhandling, homeless people can purchase copies of the newspaper, *Street News*. Then they sell the papers to passersby for a profit and pocket the difference. Each homeless worker in Persons's program also has a savings account. For every newspaper sold, a small amount of money is deposited into this account. This money is to be used later for rent. As of February 1990, over 200 homeless people saved enough from selling papers to get off the streets.[7]

People working in groups can also have an impact. In Atlanta, Georgia, a group called the "Mad Housers" has met every other week since 1987. Their goal is to build two small homes or huts by the end of each day that they meet. The huts are built—without legal permission—on abandoned public land, in wooded areas, or on empty lots. These structures become homes for homeless individuals or families. The efforts of the Mad Housers, although illegal, have put pressure on the city of Atlanta to provide adequate housing for the homeless. With few exceptions, Atlanta city officials have allowed the huts to remain.[8]

Habitat for Humanity volunteers build houses for the poor.

People involved in Habitat for Humanity are dedicated to building decent housing for the poor throughout the world. The program was started in Americus, Georgia, in 1976 by Millard Fuller, a young lawyer whose mail-order business had made him a millionaire. Since Fuller established the program, more than 3,000 houses for the poor have been built.[9] Habitat for Humanity relies on volunteer labor and donations of building materials. Former president Jimmy Carter and his wife, Rosalynn, volunteer frequently. Volunteers often give up one day a month to join a team of people who will construct a home. Homeless applicants are also part of this team, providing their own "sweat equity," or hard work, for

A newspaper hawker sells a copy of Street News *near Times Square in New York City. The homeless people who sell the paper are paid 55 cents for each issue sold.*

their homes. The families must pay for the homes over a period of years, but Habitat does not collect interest (a fee paid for borrowed money that is usually a percentage of the amount borrowed) as part of the mortgage payments.[10]

To prove that homelessness is no laughing matter, 40 comedians joined forces to make HBO's show, "Comic Relief," a success. Not only did these comedians and their hosts, Billy Crystal, Whoopi Goldberg, and Robin Williams, help raise $5 million for homeless programs such as Health Care for the Homeless, they've also kept the issue of homelessness in the public eye.[11]

Enterprising young members of the National Association of Students against Homelessness have raised over $38,000 for the needy. When law students interview for jobs, they travel to law firms across the country, and the law firm pays for the students' hotels, meals, and travel expenses. Rather than staying in luxury hotels and eating in posh restaurants, participating students stay in modest hotels and eat reasonably priced meals. The law firm donates the difference in cost to a homeless shelter. In 1989 over 150 law firms participated in this program.[12]

For many reasons already discussed, other people feel no responsibility for the homeless and their problems. Again, quoting former president Ronald Reagan, "The homeless...are homeless, you might say, by choice."[13] A large number of Americans agree with Reagan.

Almost everyone agrees on one thing—they would like to be rid of the problem of homelessness. Now that you've examined the issue, what is your opinion?

Resources to Contact

ACORN
522 Eighth Street, S.E.
Washington, D.C. 20003
202-547-9292

Catholic Charities
1319 F Street, N.W.
Washington, D.C. 20004
202-629-8400

Children's Defense Fund
122 C Street, N.W.
Washington, D.C. 20001
202-628-8787

Community for Creative Non-Violence,
  Inc.
425 Second Street, N.W.
Washington, D.C. 20001
202-393-1909

Foundation for Economic Education
30 South Broadway
Irvington, NY 10533
914-591-7230

Habitat for Humanity International
Habitat and Church Streets
Americus, GA 31709
912-924-6935

Heritage Foundation
214 Massachusetts Avenue, N.W.
Washington, D.C. 20002
202-546-4400

Homelessness Information Exchange
1830 Connecticut Avenue, N.W.
Washington, D.C. 20009
202-462-7551

National Alliance to End Homelessness
1518 K Street, N.W.
Suite 206
Washington, D.C. 20005
202-638-1526

National Coalition for the Homeless
1621 Connecticut Avenue, N.W.,
  No. 400
Washington, D.C. 20009
202-659-3310

National Housing Institute
439 Main Street
Orange, NJ 07050
201-678-3110

National Institute of Mental Health
Office of Programs for the Homeless
  Mentally Ill
5600 Fishers Lane
Rockville, MD 20857
301-443-3706

National Network of Runaway
  Youth Services
1400 I Street, N.W.
Suite 330
Washington, D.C. 20005
202-682-4114

National Student Campaign Against
  Hunger and Homelessness
29 Temple Place
Boston, MA 02111
617-292-4823

National Union of the Homeless
2001 Spring Garden Street
Philadelphia, PA 19130
215-972-7085

Salvation Army
National Public Affairs Office
1025 Vermont Avenue, N.W.
Washington, D.C. 20005
202-639-8414

Second Harvest
343 South Dearborn
Suite 410
Chicago, IL 60604
312-341-1303

United Conference of Mayors
1620 I Street, N.W.
Washington, D.C. 20005
202-293-7330

U.S. Department of Health and
  Human Services
200 Independence Avenue, S.W.
Washington, D.C. 20201
202-245-6296

U.S. Department of Housing and
  Urban Development
451 Seventh Street, S.W.
Washington, D.C. 20410
202-655-4000

U.S. House of Representatives
The Honorable Congressman or
  Congresswoman _____
Washington, D.C. 20515
202-224-3121

U.S. Senate
The Honorable Senator _____
Washington, D.C. 20510
202-224-3121

White House
President _____
1600 Pennsylvania Avenue, N.W.
Washington, D.C. 20500
202-456-1414 or 202-456-1111

Endnotes

CHAPTER 1. AN OVERVIEW

[1]Gregg Barak, *Gimme Shelter: A Social History of Homelessness in Contemporary America* (New York: Praeger, 1991), 32.

[2]Peter H. Rossi, *Down and Out in America: The Origins of Homelessness* (Chicago: University of Chicago Press, 1989), 37.

[3]Ibid.

[4]Ibid., 30-31.

[5]James D. Wright, *Address Unknown: The Homeless in America* (New York: Aldine de Gruyter, 1989), 43-44.

[6]Bureau of Labor Statistics, U.S. Department of Labor.

[7]Jonathan Kozol, *Rachel and Her Children* (New York: Crown Publishers, Inc., 1988), 11.

[8]Mary Ellen Hombs, *American Homelessness* (Santa Barbara: ABC-CLIO, Inc., 1990), 9-10.

[9]Richard Matthews, "A Tragic Harvest," *Country Journal*, September/October 1989, 10.

[10]Rossi, 40-41.

[11]Mary Ellen Hombs and Mitch Snyder, *Homelessness in America: A Forced March to Nowhere* (Washington, D.C.: Community for Creative Non-Violence, 1983), 9.

[12]*Homelessness in America: A Summary* (Washington, D.C.: National Coalition for the Homeless, n.d.), 2.

[13]Rossi, 42-43.

[14]Joel Blau, The Visible Poor: Homelessness in the United States (New York: Oxford University Press, 1992), 29.

[15]Sarah Ferguson, "Us vs. Them: America's Growing Frustration with the Homeless," *Utne Reader* (excerpted from the Pacific News Service), September/October 1990, 53.

CHAPTER 2. THE CAUSES OF HOMELESSNESS

[1]Pam, interview with author, Albuquerque, New Mexico, November 1991. All further attributions to "Pam" are based on this interview. The names of the homeless people that appear in this book have all been changed to protect their privacy.

[2]*The World Almanac and Book of Facts 1992* (New York: Scripps Howard, 1992), 134.

[3]Milton Meltzer, *Poverty in America* (New York: William Morrow, 1986), 41.

[4]Kozol, 13.

[5]Ibid., 209.

[6]Peter Marin, "How We Help and Harm the Homeless," *Utne Reader* (excerpted from *Harper's*), January/February, 46.

[7]John Huey, "How We Can Win the War on Poverty," *Fortune*, April 10, 1989, 128.

[8]*Housing and Homelessness: A Teaching Guide* (Washington, D.C.: Housing Now, 1989), 28.

[9]"Handy Reference Guide to the Fair Labor Standards Act" (Washington, D.C.: U.S. Department of Labor, April 1990).

[10]*Summary*, 2-3.

[11]Ibid., 3.

[12]Wright, 81.

[13]Rossi, 43.

[14]*The Problem of Homelessness* (Washington, D.C.: Homelessness Exchange, n.d.), 1.

[15]*Summary,* 4.

[16]Ibid.

[17]Ibid.

[18]Lisa Orr, ed., *The Homeless* (San Diego: Greenhaven Press, 1990), 115.

[19]Marin, 40-41.

[20]Johnson, 154.

[21]*Summary,* 2.

[22]*Problems of Homelessness,* 2.

[23]Ibid.

CHAPTER 3. "THREE HOTS AND A COT"

[1]*Fact Sheet.*

[2]Elaine Landau, *The Homeless* (New York: Julian Messner, 1987), 39-40.

[3]Ibid., 40.

[4]Orr, 48-49.

[5]Edward Barnes, "The Can People: From Urban Trash Bins, A New Currency—Aluminum," *Life,* August 1989, 98-99.

CHAPTER 4. HOMELESS CHILDREN AND THEIR FAMILIES

[1]Marjorie J. Robertson and Milton Greenblatt, *Homelessness: A National Perspective* (New York: Plenum Press, 1992), 235.

[2]Kozol, 3.

[3]Ibid., 4.

[4]Ibid., 82.

[5]Joan J. Johnson, *Kids Without Homes* (New York: Franklin Watts, 1991), 61.

[6]Kozol, 169.

[7]Johnson, 63.

[8]Peggy McIntire, executive director of Cuidando Los Niños, interview with author, November 1991. All other attributions to Peggy McIntire are based on this interview.

[9]Kozol, 87.

[10]Johnson, 84.

[11]Wright, 120.

CHAPTER 5. HOMELESS OR HOPELESS?

[1]James G., interview with author, November 1991. All other attributions to James G. are based on this interview.

[2]Orr, 115.

[3]Ferguson, 54.

[4]Steven V. Roberts, "Reagan on Homelessness: Many Choose to Live in the Streets," *New York Times,* December 22, 1988.

[5]Orr, 114.

[6]Ibid.

[7]Ibid., 115.

[8]Ibid., 101.

[9]Ferguson, 51.

[10]Ibid.

[11]Kozol, 178.

[12]Ibid.

[13]Ibid., 177-178.

[14]Isabel Wilkerson, "Shift in Feelings on the Homeless: Empathy Turns to Frustration," *New York Times*, September 2, 1991, 1.

[15]Rossi, 190.

[16]Orr, 114.

[17]Marsha McMurray-Avila, executive director of Health Care for the Homeless, Albuquerque, New Mexico, and board member of the National Coalition for the Homeless, interview with author, January 1991. All other attributions to Marsha McMurray-Avila are based on this interview.

[18]*Summary*, 1.

[19]"Homeless in Poor Mental, Physical Health," *Science News*, November 4, 1991, 302.

[20]*A Commitment to End Homelessness* (Washington, D.C.: National Coalition for the Homeless, n.d.), 3.

[21]Hilary Stout, "Health Care Choices: A Bigger Federal Role or a Market Approach?" *The Wall Street Journal*, February 6, 1992, 1.

[22]Daniel S. Levy, "A Beacon on Lonely Street," *Time*, December 17, 1991, 14-18.

[23]*A Commitment to End Homelessness*, 1.

[24]Al Santoli, "Your Brothers Are Here," *Parade*, October 13, 1991, 12.

[25]David Whitman, "The Return of Skid Row: Why Alcoholics and Drug Addicts Are Filling the Streets Again," *U.S. News and World Report*, January 15, 1990, 29.

[26]Wright, 153.

[27]Johnson, 145.

[28]Landau, 89.

St. Martin's Project Care, (Albuquerque, New Mexico, n.d.), pamphlet.

[30]McMurray-Avila interview.

[31]David Whitman, "Hope for the Homeless," *U.S. News and World Report*, February 29, 1988, 34.

[32]Wright, 141-142.

[33]Whitman, "Hope for the Homeless," 34.

[34]Johnson, 141.

[35]Orr, 196.

[36]Wright, 147.

[37]Kozol, 203.

[38]Landau, 91.

[39]Barak, 168.

[40]Ibid., 169.

[41]Ibid.

[42]Rossi, 35.

[43]Barak, 169.

[44]Ibid.

[45]Orr, 125-126.

[46]Barak, 169.

CHAPTER 6. PIECES OF THE PUZZLE

[1]*Fact Sheet.*

[2]Joan Johnson, *Kids Without Homes* (New York: Franklin Watts, 1991), 14.

[3]Paul W. Cohen, "One Teen's Campaign for the Homeless," *Scholastic Update,* February 10, 1989, 20-22.

[4]David Brand, "One Heart Warms Many Chilly Fingers," *Time,* January 2, 1989, 16.

[5]Colman McCarthy, "Mitch Snyder," *The Nation,* July 30/August 6, 1990, 116.

[6]Sue Allison, "Street Tent," *Life,* June 1989, 7.

[7]Leslie Whitaker, "Helping Them Help Themselves," *Time,* February 29, 1990, 56.

[8]Montgomery Brower, "Gimme Shelter? Atlanta's Mad Housers Are Heeding the Plea," *People,* May 9, 1988, 116.

[9]Thomas L. Kenyon, *What You Can Do to Help the Homeless* (New York: Simon and Schuster, 1991), 72.

[10]Huey, 124.

[11]Ellen Whitford, "Filling the Gaps," *Scholastic Update,* February 10, 1989, 19.

[12]Peter Nulty, "Harvard Law's Pro Bono Students," *Fortune,* December 18, 1989, 8.

[13]Orr, 13.

Glossary

doubling up: moving in with a family member or friend

gentrification: the migration of middle-class people into a deteriorated area; the process of turning a run-down area into an area of stylish homes and businesses

housing subsidies: money the government gives to the poor to assist with rental payments

inflation: an increase in the volume of money and credit relative to available goods, resulting in a substantial and continuing rise in the general price level

minimum wage: a wage fixed by law as the lowest wage permitted to be paid to employed persons

panhandler: someone who stops people on the street to ask them for money

poverty line: a level of personal or family income below which one is classified as poor according to government standards

Skid Row: a district of cheap bars and single-room occupancy hotels frequented by vagrants and substance abusers

soup kitchen: an establishment that provides minimal meals to the needy

squatter: one who settles on property without right or rental payment

SRO: a single-room occupancy hotel that offers small rooms at cheap prices

transients: people who move frequently from one place to another, usually in search of work or better conditions

underemployed: those who have less than full-time hours or regular jobs, or work at jobs that are inadequate with respect to their training or economic needs

warehousing: a term used to describe a condition in which many people sleep in one large room

Bibliography

Aeschliman, M. D., and Ian Whitehead. "No More Shacks: Habitat for Humanity." *National Review,* December 30, 1988, 40.

Allison, Sue. "Street Tent." *Life,* June 1989, 7.

Bader, Eleanor J. "The 'Housing Now!' March on Washington." *Humanist,* January/February 1990, 5.

Baggot, Teresa. "'Nightmare Year' Wrenches Family from Dream Home." *National Catholic Reporter,* March 8, 1991, 6.

Baker, James N. "Don't Sleep in the Subway; Beggars Beware: Cities Crack Down on Vagrants." *Newsweek,* June 24, 1991, 26.

Barak, Gregg. *Gimme Shelter: A Social History of Homelessness in Contemporary America.* New York: Praeger, 1991.

Barnes, Edward. "The Can People: From Urban Trash Bins, a New Currency—Aluminum." *Life,* August 1989, 98.

Beckelman, Laurie. *The Homeless.* New York: Crestwood House, Macmillan Publishing Co., 1989.

Bidinotto, Robert James. "Myths about the Homeless." *Reader's Digest,* June 1991, 98.

Blau, Joel. The Visible Poor: Homelessness in the United States. New York: Oxford University Press, 1992.

Brand, David. "One Heart Warms Many Chilly Fingers." *Time,* January 2, 1989, 16.

Brower, Montgomery. "Gimme Shelter? Atlanta's Mad Housers Are Heeding the Plea." *People,* May 9, 1988, 116.

"CDBG Help—From the Shelter to the Workplace." *Nation's Cities,* March 13, 1989, 11.

Cohen, Paul W. "One Teen's Campaign for the Homeless." *Scholastic Update,* February 10, 1989, 20.

A Commitment to End Homelessness. Washington, D.C.: National Coalition for the Homeless, October 1990.

"The Countless Homeless." *National Review,* April 16, 1990, 15.

Dudley, William, ed. *Poverty.* St. Paul, Minn.: Greenhaven Press, 1988.

"The Dynamics of Homelessness." *Children Today,* May/June 1989, 2.

Ferrell, Frank, and Janet Ferrell. *Trevor's Place.* San Francisco: Harper & Row, 1985.

Gelman, David. "Some Really Good Scouts: For Homeless Girls—a Troop to Call Their Own." *Newsweek,* January 14, 1991, 58.

"Global Strategy for Shelter to the Year 2000 Adopted: Poor and Homeless Are Its Main Focus." *UN Chronicle,* September 1988, 64.

Hombs, Mary Ellen. *American Homelessness.* Santa Barbara, Calif.: ABC-CLIO, Inc., 1990.

Hombs, Mary Ellen, and Mitch Snyder. *Homelessness in America: A Forced March to Nowhere.* Washington, D.C.: Community for Creative Non-Violence, 1983.

"Homeless in Poor Mental, Physical Health." *Science News,* November 4, 1989, 302.

"Homeless in the Land of Enchantment." *Albuquerque Monthly,* December 1990, 1-15.

Homelessness in America: A Summary. Washington, D.C.: National Coalition for the Homeless, February 1991.

Housing and Homelessness: A Teaching Guide. Washington, D.C.: Housing Now, 1989.

Huey, John, and David Kirkpatrick. "How We Can Win the War on Poverty." *Fortune,* April 10, 1989, 124.

Johnson, Joan J. *Kids Without Homes.* New York: Franklin Watts, 1991.

Jones, Peter M. "Four Causes of Homelessness." *Scholastic Update,* February 10, 1989, 12.

Kenyon, Thomas L. *What You Can Do to Help the Homeless.* New York: Simon and Schuster, 1991.

Kessler, Brad. "The Homeless Movement: After Charity, Start Organizing." *The Nation,* April 16, 1988, 528.

King, Charles E. "Homelessness in America." *The Humanist,* May/June 1989, 8.

King, Johanna. "Agency's Programs Helping Many Turn Around Health, Lives." *Albuquerque Journal,* November 18, 1991.

King, Patricia. "Help for the Homeless; Cities and Private Investors Fight to Save Single-Room Occupancy Hotels." *Newsweek,* April 11, 1989, 58.

Kosof, Anna. *Homeless in America.* New York: Franklin Watts, 1988.

Koyanagi, Chris. "Homelessness: What Is the Federal Government Doing?" *National Mental Health Association Speaks,* January 17, 1989.

Kozol, Jonathan. *Rachel and Her Children.* New York: Crown Publishers, Inc., 1988.

Landau, Elaine. *The Homeless.* New York: Julian Messner, 1987.

Lave, Judith R. "Band-Aid Solutions." *Society,* May/June 1989, 11.

Leo, John. "Homeless Rights, Community Wrongs." *U.S. News and World Report,* July 24, 1989, 56.

Levy, Daniel S. "A Beacon on Lonely Street: Planned Parenthood's Street Beat Vans Bring Health Care and a Ray of Hope to the Down-and-Out Kids of the Bronx." *Time,* December 17, 1990, 14.

McCarthy, Colman. "Mitch Snyder." *The Nation,* July 30/August 6, 1990, 116.

Main, Thomas J. "What We Know About the Homeless." *Commentary,* May 1988, 26.

Manning, Steven. "Is the Government Doing Enough to End Homelessness?" *Scholastic Update,* February 10, 1989, 14.

Marcus, Naomi, Vivica Novak, and James Romanesko. "The Many Faces of America's Homeless." *Scholastic Update,* February 10, 1989, 9.

Matthews, Richard. "A Tragic Harvest." *Country Journal,* September/October 1989, 10.

Meltzer, Milton. *Poverty in America.* New York: William Morrow and Co., 1986.

Miller, Mark, Jennifer Foote, Patricia King, Mariana Gosenell, and Tom Mathews, "What Can Be Done?" *Newsweek,* March 21, 1988, 57.

Mundell, Lynn. "Fresh Ideas for Dealing with the Homeless Crisis." *Nation's Cities*, April 11, 1988, 6.

Needle, Charles. "Finding a Home for the Homeless." *American City and County*, December 1988, 40.

Nulty, Peter. "Harvard Law's Pro Bono Students." *Fortune*, December 18, 1989, 8.

O'Connor, Patricia. "Home Base for the Homeless." *Albuquerque Monthly*, December 1990, 5.

Orr, Lisa, ed. *The Homeless*. San Diego: Greenhaven Press, Inc., 1990.

Peirce, Neal R. "Giving Up on Public Housing Ought to Be Unthinkable." *Nation's Cities*, September 11, 1989, 8.

The Problem of Homelessness. Homelessness Exchange. Pamphlet.

Relin, David Oliver. "Lives on Hold." *Scholastic Update*, February 10, 1989, 5.

Relin, David Oliver. "Lost to the Streets." *Scholastic Update*, January 25, 1991, 10.

Rossi, Peter H. *Down and Out in America: The Origins of Homelessness*. Chicago: University of Chicago Press, 1989.

Rubenstein, Ed. "How Many Homeless?" *National Review*, May 14, 1990, 17.

Santoli, Al. "Your Brothers Are Here." *Parade Magazine*, October 13, 1991, 12.

Teitelbaum, Richard S. "Companies That Feed the Homeless." *Fortune*, November 6, 1989, 10.

"They Count at Night." *Time*, February 5, 1990, 25.

"To Help the Homeless, Comedy's Heaviest Hitters Cheerfully Pitched Relief and Raised $7.5 million." *People*, May 28, 1990, 83.

Vago, Elizabeth. "The Homeless: What Can We Do?" *Nation's Cities*, December 17, 1990, 11.

Whitaker, Leslie. "Helping Them Help Themselves: A New Publication Tries to Get the Homeless off the Street." *Time*, February 26, 1990, 56.

Whitford, Ellen. "Filling the Gaps." *Scholastic Update*, February 10, 1989, 18.

Whitman, David. "Hope for the Homeless." *U.S. News and World Report*. February 29, 1988, 25.

Whitman, David. "The Return of Skid Row: Why Alcoholics and Addicts Are Filling the Streets Again." *U.S. News and World Report*, January 15, 1990, 27.

Woodrum, Pat. "A Haven for the Homeless." *Library Journal*, January 1988, 55.

"The Word on the Street." *Time*, December 4, 1989, 69.

Wright, James D. "Address Unknown: Homelessness in Contemporary America." *Society*, September/October 1989, 45.

Wright, James D. *Address Unknown: The Homeless in America*. New York: Aldine de Gruyter, 1989.

Index

Index (continued)

• •

Acknowledgements

AP/Wide World Photos, 11 (bottom), 45, 46, 100; Bettmann Archive, 11 (top);
Carlye Calvin, 74 (top); COMEA, 83; Ford Motor Company, 27 (bottom);
Habitat for Humanity, Inc., 99; Jeffrey High/Image Productions, 10, 17, 19, 40,
47, 54 (both), 59, 66 (botom), 84 (bottom); Jim Hubbard, 6, 30, 48, 52, 53, 57
(both), 68, 70, 74 (bottom), 86, 90, 94; Independent Picture Service, 55;
Thomas Ives, 14, 15, 22, 31, 36, 41, 45 (top), 61, 64, 66 (top), 71, 78; Minneapolis
Public Library and Information Center, 56; Tara C. Patty, 39, 80, 84 (top);
Skjold Photographs, front cover, 25, 89; Joseph Sorrentino, 51, 73, 98; UPI/
Bettmann, 63; White Castle System, Inc. 27 (top); W. Bryan Winget, 20, 69.